New Mexico
on my mind

The
Globe
Pequot
Press

Guilford, Connecticut

Library of Congress Number: 90-80038

ISBN 1-56044-034-1

Manufactured in Korea
First Edition/Fifth Printing

Front cover photos
SCOTT T. SMITH *Yucca on dunes at White Sands
  National Monument*
STEPHEN TRIMBLE *Acoma Pueblo pot*

Back cover photos
RANDALL K. ROBERTS *Albuquerque International
  Balloon Festival*
RANDALL K. ROBERTS *Whooping crane and sandhill
  cranes at Bosque del Apache National Wildlife Refuge*
STEPHEN TRIMBLE *Comanche dancer at San Juan Pueblo*

Paintbrush and badlands in the Angel Peak area east of Farmington   KENT & DONNA DANNEN

introduction

There are two ways to become a New Mexican, according to Oliver La Farge: by birth or by passionate adoption.

Mine was by passionate adoption. And, as immigrants do, I often reflect on my adopted home, trying to determine how this place worked its way so deeply into my soul that when someone asks about New Mexico, I don't hesitate to use the word "love" to describe my feelings.

It wasn't love at first sight. Some immigrants succumb to New Mexico's allure immediately, but when I first came here more than twenty years ago from the Midwest, passionate adoption was a long way off.

New Mexico's primary color—brown—was all wrong to my Midwestern eyes. The houses—flat-roofed, adobe, or more likely stucco designed to look like adobe—were wrong. The shape of the land—immense, flat in one direction, mountainous in another—was wrong.

It took a year, maybe two, before I looked around and thought: *I don't want to leave this place.*

What happened? To this day I'm not sure. There was no great thunderous awakening. There was no single incident that crystallized the thought. Nothing dominated, just as no single fact of geography or demography dominates New Mexico.

New Mexico had simply seeped into my soul. The process was subtle, a series of shadings, of discoveries, that coalesced one day into the thought that has anchored my feelings about New Mexico for years now: *I don't want to leave this place.*

Maybe it happened in July or August, in what we call the "monsoon season," when fierce twenty-minute storms sweep across the high desert, drench the land, and cause us to stop to watch the rain.

New Mexico's climate is dry, with long but infrequent nurturing rains—"female" rains the Indian people call them—and short, violent summer storms—the "male rains."

When rain comes, irrespective of its gender, we watch. At home, at work, no matter where we might be at the moment the rain falls, we stop to relish the moment. Umbrellas are collectors' items in New Mexico, odd conversation pieces. Avoiding rain isn't in our psyches. We tend to seek it out.

So I might have settled on New Mexico the day I noticed I had begun to savor rain. Or it might have been on a winter morning in one of Albuquerque's rare snowstorms, when I realized that I was an expert snow driver only in the snow of my memory.

New Mexicans take a lot of abuse from veterans of snowy climates. I used to be one of the abusers, giving my native New Mexican wife hours of grief over New Mexicans' predictable panic at the sight of a snow flurry. Then one day I noticed that my car was slipping and sliding on the most modest of snowfalls. And I stopped reminding her of how a little snow never bothered a true snow driver.

When did I become a New Mexican? No single answer presents itself. No lone element grabbed me by the lapels and shouted, "Here! I'm New Mexico! Understand this and you'll have a handle on the whole place!" But to understand New Mexico, we must begin somewhere. So let's start with the land.

There's a lot of it. New Mexico is the fifth largest state in the nation, 122,666 square miles populated by a little more than one million people. That works out to eight people per square mile. If it's solitude you want, you don't have to look far here.

The Southern Rockies come down from Colorado into the high country of northern New Mexico and end in the central Rio Grande Valley. Many of the names given to various mountain ranges by the Spanish explorers

Sage advice EDWARD WORMAN

reflect a common theme—red. There are the Sangre de Cristo (Blood of Christ), Sandia (Watermelon), Manzano (Apple). When the setting sun splashes crimson across these ranges, the names become self-explanatory.

Seven New Mexico mountains rise higher than 13,000 feet. Many more top 10,000. The plains of Texas roll into New Mexico's east side but then surrender to those mountains in the center of the state. In the south, the Sonoran Desert rises from Mexico, but it too succumbs to the altitude.

All of these areas comprise the state; none of them alone defines it. Each piece of New Mexico has its own beauty. Some places are breathtaking; others are stark, such as the Jornado del Muerte (Journey of Death) in southern New Mexico, which attracts the eye with its frightening austerity. It seems nothing could live here, that it is indeed a dead place. But go out into it and you'll find life—gritty vegetation clinging to barren soil, hardy animals that have found a home in the harshness.

Go from one end of New Mexico to the other and you go from alpine peaks to the farmland of the Rio Grande Valley, from the brisk temperatures along the Continental Divide to the flaming heat of the Sonoran Desert.

Even in Albuquerque, the state's largest city with almost half a million people, you can feel the presence of the land. Stuck in traffic at a busy intersection, I can see it, no matter what direction I choose to look. It beckons in the changing colors of the sky, summer storms sweeping across the horizon, blues and reds swirling together to produce colors the mind cannot imagine. Out in that great space is peace.

Edward Abbey once wrote, "Walk one-half mile away from the town, away from the road, and you find yourself absolutely alone, under the sun, under the moon, under the stars, within the sweet aching loneliness of the desert."

He could have been writing of Albuquerque, where a fifteen-minute drive from the city limits will take you out into the expanse. You will be swallowed by it, dwarfed by it, and not at all displeased with the swift journey that brought you face to face with your own insignificance.

If I were asked to name a favorite place in New Mexico, I'd probably say, "Well, this one . . . and that one, and that one, and probably these two." Then I'd get down to some serious equivocation.

I like the High Road to Taos. It begins north of Santa Fe, off the main highway that twists through the Rio Grande Canyon on its way to Taos and the Rio Grande Gorge. The High Road winds through villages established by the colonial Spanish to protect Santa Fe from Comanche war parties: Truchas, Chimayo, Las Trampas, and all the rest that give you the notion the Spanish colonial empire in America might not be as far removed as history books suggest. Adobe churches built before the American Revolution still stand and still are used. Old age is a given in New Mexico.

I've been across the High Road to Taos many times. I never tire of its magic. But its mysteries do not hold universal appeal. I once took a newcomer to New Mexico across the High Road. He was a native of Ohio and had never been out West. We passed jagged peaks and small green valleys dotted with homes and livestock. We slowed at the old adobe houses, some chocolate brown, some tan, some white, an occasional pink. The landscape surrounding each was unchanged ten yards from the house, and fifty yards, and eight hundred yards. As far as we could see, the land was brown, harsh, breathtaking, and speckled with pinyon trees and squat, tough vegetation hanging on to the dry land for dear life. The owners of the houses had not tamed the land. Much of New Mexico's land does not submit easily to domestication.

In this place rich in history, peopled by the descendants of conquistadors and ancient Indian tribes, the newcomer from Ohio said, "You'd think people would want to clean up their yards and plant a little grass."

I understood. Some people never get used to it.

So I like the High Road to Taos. It's one of my favorites. But then I like the Jemez, too.

The Jemez Mountains lie about an hour and a half northwest of Albuquerque. They are marked by red rock and steep canyon walls. To get to the Jemez from Albuquerque, you turn off the interstate onto Highway 44 and pass through the village of Bernalillo. At the crest of a series of gentle but escalating rises in the desert, the northern horizon explodes into a mind-boggling display of distant mountains, ridge lines drifting in and out of a powder-blue haze, arroyos gouged by years of flash floods, and mesas cutting across the sky as if they'd been drawn with a straight-edge.

When I travel south, I enjoy Sierra Blanca, whitecapped in winter, jutting gray in summer;

Feathers and friars   STEPHEN SIMPSON

Lincoln County, Billy the Kid and Pat Garrett country, with its history of violence and pitched battles between warring ranch empires; and the Tularosa Basin, empty enough to hold a secret as explosive as the first detonation of an atomic bomb. In the Tularosa Basin is that strip of otherworldliness we call White Sands, acres not of sand but of gypsum, molded by the wind into an endless series of dunes.

If I head still farther south, I come to the Carlsbad Caverns, deep in the earth's innards, the temperature constantly cool regardless of the surface conditions' vagaries.

Each place is different, each adds to the whole, but none claims supremacy over the rest.

The people who live in this landscape are every bit as diverse as the land. Generally, if you want to find us, it's best to look outside. We spend a lot of time fishing, hiking, camping, skiing (downhill and cross-country), biking, walking, and flying hot-air balloons. Just about any excuse to go outside will do. We have the space and we have the weather.

What I like best about New Mexico's people is their variety. When the great wave of Anglo settlers spread across the West, there wasn't much to draw them to New Mexico. So rather than wash over the established cultures of the West as they did in so many other places, those who came to New Mexico tended to blend in with those who had been here before them: the Spanish, the Mexican, the Navajo, the Apache, the nineteen Pueblo tribes.

As the cultures blended but still maintained enough independence to survive, New Mexico evolved its own unique music, rituals, and food. We speak English, Spanish, and several Indian languages.

My favorite cultural crossroads is Christmas. Each Christmas Eve, I walk the plaza of Old Town in Albuquerque, surrounded by *luminarias,* the gentle lights that mark this special night in New Mexico.

Tradition has it that these thousands of small paper bags with their flickering candles light the way for the Christ Child. They line every sidewalk, every adobe wall, every rooftop of every building. They spread across the plaza and into the courtyard of the San Felipe de Neri Church. They stretch into the surrounding neighborhoods, gentle signals of peace on this special night. *Luminarias* flicker everywhere in New Mexico on Christmas Eve.

The night often ends with a visit to a friend's house for conversation and food that is always marked by that singular New Mexico contribution to world cuisine: chile.

In Texas, they call it "chili" and it is brown and mushy. In New Mexico, we call it "chile"

and it comes in two colors: red and green. If, after two bites, tears well up in your eyes and your nose runs and your sinuses clear up for the first time in years, you are not eating Texas chili. You aren't even eating Mexican food. You are eating New Mexican food, a unique blend of Mexican and Indian traditions.

New Mexico's uniqueness does have its price: An alarming number of Americans don't know who or where we are. The state tourism bureau receives hundreds of calls each year from apprehensive Americans: Do they need passports to enter New Mexico? Do they need shots to ward off exotic diseases? Does New Mexico accept American dollars? Are tours conducted with English-speaking guides? And the classic: Is the water safe to drink?

It never ends. Year after year, the geography-impaired place New Mexico squarely in Latin America. Consider these examples:

— When an Ohio man received a top secret clearance from the federal government, he was given a list of foreign countries considered hostile to the United States. New Mexico was on the list.

— New Mexico State University tried to place some of its graduates in jobs at the U.S. Department of Energy. A personnel specialist in the DOE's Chicago office wrote back: "We suggest you inquire about citizenship requirements for federal employment."

— A newspaper reporter moving from Kansas to New Mexico told a friend about the move.

Christmas lights and *luminarias* STEPHEN SIMPSON

"But you've already been in the Peace Corps," the friend said. "Why do you have to go back?"

We shake our heads in wonder: How can people do this? How can they misplace a whole state?

Maybe in part it's because we call New Mexico the Land of Enchantment, which implies mystery. Mysteries take time to solve, even if the evidence is right there under your nose, let alone thousands of miles away. Maybe people just haven't taken the time to understand us.

A friend of mine, a longstanding New Mexican by way of passionate adoption, once took a train trip from Albuquerque to El Paso. He sat near three Midwestern travelers. About thirty miles out of Albuquerque, the train slowly climbed out of a long gentle depression in the land. As it reached the crest of a small hill, the three Midwesterners looked out the window. To the west, the high desert spread into infinity under a blue sky that left no question about why the ancient ones of New Mexico put such value on turquoise. Eighty miles away, a mountain towered across the horizon. It is called Mount Taylor on the maps, but it has other names: Turquoise Mountain and Tso Dzil. It is one of the Navajo holy places, secured to the ground by a magic stone knife, decorated with turquoise, blue cloud, and female rain, and protected by Big Snake. When the Hero Twins—Monster Slayer and Child Born of Water—made the land safe for people, they began their quest at Turquoise Mountain.

"Look at that!" one of the travelers said.

My friend recalls that his chest swelled with pride. He was about to introduce himself, maybe start a friendly conversation about New Mexico, when another of the Midwesterners caused him to sit back and keep quiet.

"Yeah," the second traveler said. "Why would anybody want to live in a place like this?"

It's a fair question. The elusive answer lies somewhere in the words of Oliver La Farge: "What is New Mexico, then? How sum it up? It is a vast, harsh, poverty-stricken, varied, and beautiful land, breeder of artists and warriors. It is the home, by birth or by passionate adoption, of a wildly assorted population which has shown itself capable of achieving homogeneity without sacrificing its diversity. It is primitive, undeveloped, overused, new, raw, rich with tradition, old, and mellow. It is a land full of the essence of peace, although its history is one of invasions and conflicts. It is itself, an entity, at times infuriating, at times utterly delightful to its lovers, a land that draws and holds men and women with ties that cannot be explained or submitted to reason."

Yes, this is New Mexico. *I don't want to leave this place.*

Jim Arnholz
Albuquerque

Day's end at Penasco Blanco, Anasazi ruins at Chaco Culture National Historical Park   SCOTT T. SMITH

Acoma Pueblo, continuously inhabited since the twelfth century, as seen from San Estevan del Rey Mission   TERRENCE MOORE

Isleta Pueblo mission church, parts dating to 1613, one of the oldest mission churches in the nation   GREG RYAN / SALLY BEYER

The altar of El Sanctuario de Chimayo, sometimes called "the Lourdes of the Southwest"   A PLACE

Thirteenth-century Mogollon Indian ruins at Gila Cliff Dwellings National Monument   LAURENCE PARENT

" *And here . . . the two great questions are 'Where did they come from? Where did they go?' You ask with tiredness and resignation, for there is no answer. Nobody knows.* **"**

Ernie Pyle,
Ernie Pyle's Southwest

Anasazi petroglyph (rock carving) in Galisteo Basin,
southeast of Santa Fe   STEPHEN TRIMBLE

Ruins of Pueblo Bonito, once a 650-room Anasazi community, now a ghost town in Chaco Canyon   LARRY ULRICH

Lower Frijoles Canyon, Bandelier National Monument   ED COOPER

" . . . in the midst of that wavy ocean of sand, was a green thread of verdure and a running stream. This ribbon in the desert seemed no wider than a man could throw a stone,—and it was greener than anything Latour had ever seen . . . . "

Willa Cather,
Death Comes for the Archbishop

Upper Falls in Frijoles Canyon, south of Los Alamos   WILLARD CLAY

Sunrise over the Organ Mountains, east of Las Cruces   WILLARD CLAY

> " *. . . perfectly mad looking country—hills and cliffs and washes too crazy to imagine all thrown up into the air by God and let tumble where they would.* "

Georgia O'Keeffe,
Letter to Alfred Stieglitz, 1937

The Chama River, a tributary of the Rio Grande, near Abiquiu   RANDALL K. ROBERTS

A bumper crop of chile peppers, the state vegetable SUZI S. MOORE

Garfield chile grower with samples of his wares, loose and hanging in ristra SUZI S. MOORE

Fine fruits and chiles for sale in Chimayo STEPHEN SIMPSON

Handcrafted Indian rugs and pottery in an Old Town gallery, Albuquerque   A PLACE

" There is a design in living things; their shapes, forms, the ability to live, all have meaning. We must cling to our Indian traditions which exalt beauty . . . : all we can say is that we have a way of life, and that this is life itself. "

Popovi Da,
quoted in The Pueblo Indians

Feast Day at Santa Clara Pueblo   STEPHEN TRIMBLE

Navajo woman in traditional silver concho belt and turquoise and silver bracelet   STEPHEN TRIMBLE

Indian market at the Palace of Governors, Santa Fe Plaza
BRIAN PARKER / TOM STACK & ASSOCIATES

Distinctive Navajo wool rug   TERRENCE MOORE

> " *...there is something magical about New Mexico that drives people to create.* "

R. Conrad Stein,
America the Beautiful: New Mexico

Santa Clara Pueblo artist with sample of her work   STEPHEN TRIMBLE

Wall mural, Silver City   HIRAM L. PARENT

Handcrafted clay figurine   STEPHEN TRIMBLE

Seventeenth-century Pecos Indian pottery superimposed over ruins at Pecos National Monument   DAVID MUENCH

Siesta in Mesilla   TERRENCE MOORE

Hispanic hat trick in Taos   BUDDY MAYS

Hispanic homemaker in Santa Fe   BUDDY MAYS

Sunset over Inscription Rock, El Morro National Monument   FRED HIRSCHMANN

“ *I take possession, once, twice, and thrice, and all the times I can and must, of the . . .kingdom and province of New Mexico.* **”**

Don Juan de Onate,
establishing the first Spanish colony in New Mexico, 1598

Zuni pictograph (rock painting) near the Village of the Great Kivas ruins, Zuni Indian Reservation   FRED HIRSCHMANN

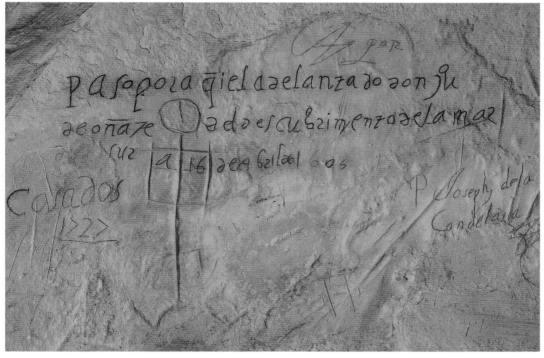

Onate inscription dated "the 16th of April of 1605," El Morro National Monument   ED COOPER

It is the land that holds us here. It is the unrelenting land, this great, fierce, challenging, canyon-gutted, mesa-muscled land, which holds us and which gives us space enough to write a life on—and leaves it to us whether we have courage enough and faith to fill the page.

John DeWitt McKee,
New Mexico Quarterly

Summer storm over Jemez Canyon, west of Santa Fe   ED COOPER

Early morning light on radiating dike and distant Shiprock   DONALD N. LESKE

“ The natural mystery of plains giving back to the sky a second sunlight and of mountains drawing the horizon up to blue pinnacles dazzled men through three hundred years, and led them up the dry beds of creeks and over the heat lakes toward the Cities of Cibola, whose yellow gates they never found....What wealth they ever found in that land was created by man with the earth, and toiled for in obedience to the seasons. ”

Paul Horgan,
Far from Cibola

Towering Shiprock, keystone of the Navajo faith   RON SANFORD

Wildflower carpet in the Sacramento Mountains, on the Lincoln National Forest   LAURENCE PARENT

Glorieta Mesa on the Santa Fe National Forest, southeast of Santa Fe   GEORGE H. H. HUEY

Bugling bull elk JAN L. WASSINK

Black bear, the state animal JEFF FOOTT

Mule deer buck   DENNIS HENRY

Crimson maples along Big Dry Creek in the 558,000-acre Gila Wilderness PETER KRESAN

Wind-battered Douglas-fir atop Sandia Crest, northeast of Albuquerque   LAURENCE PARENT

Winter blanket over Sandia Crest, on the Cibola National Forest   DAVID MUENCH

A storm brewing over Baldy Peak in the Sangre de Cristo Mountains   WILLARD CLAY

" *Weather tumbles out of the mountains just as it rolls off the changing sea. Like the sea, these mountains can be dangerous, sudden, inexplicable—they can engulf and kill easily, then roll over and seem as gentle and as compassionate as a summer meadow: and you wonder how ever you could have feared them.* "

John Nichols,
If Mountains Die

Skiing amid snow ghosts in the Sandia Mountains just outside Albuquerque   RANDALL K. ROBERTS

Striking out cross-country   KEN GALLARD

Evidence of a day's play at Taos Ski Valley KEN GALLARD

Casting for trout at Kathryn Lake, one of fifteen fishing lakes in the Pecos Wilderness   BUDDY MAYS

> *We seem always to have attracted that unmaterialistic minority that values empty places, silences, and big sky more than the power and the glory.*

Tony Hillerman,
American West

A rafting river's revenge—the famous Box Run on the Rio Grande KEN GALLARD

Backpacking at Bandelier SCOTT T. SMITH

Annual balloon rally at Red Rock State Park, east of Gallup   RANDALL K. ROBERTS

Standouts at the Albuquerque International Balloon Festival   ROBERT W. LIENEMANN

Building bubbles at White Sands National Monument   SCOTT T. SMITH

❝ *There is nothing like the White Sands anywhere in the world. They are an albino Sahara. They are miles of drifted sugar. They are an ocean of utter white. They astound you and give you the creeps.* **❞**

Ernie Pyle,
Ernie Pyle's Southwest

Hardy golden-leaved cottonwood at White Sands National Monument   LAURENCE PARENT

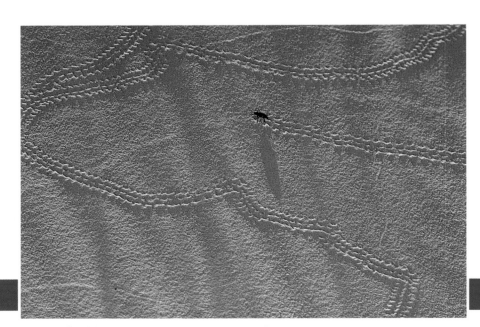

Darkling beetle and tracks at White Sands   GLENN VAN NIMWEGEN

Hiking at sunset at White Sands National Monument southwest of Alamogordo   RANDALL K. ROBERTS

> **"** *Go as far as you dare in the heart of a lonely land, you cannot go so far that life and death are not before you. Painted lizards slip in and out of rock crevices, and pant on the white hot sands. Birds, hummingbirds even, nest in the cactus scrub; woodpeckers befriend the demoniac yuccas; out of the stark, treeless waste rings the music of the night-singing mockingbird. If it be summer and the sun well down, there will be a burrowing owl to call. Strange, furry, tricksy things dart across open places, or sit motionless in the conning towers of the creosote.... They are nearly all night workers, finding the days too hot and white.* **"**

Mary Austin,
The Land of Little Rain

Dusk-blue dunes of White Sands, at 144,000 acres the largest gypsum desert in the world   GLENN VAN NIMWEGEN

Hoodoos in the Ah-Shi-Sle-Pah Wilderness Study Area near Chaco Canyon   RON SANFORD

Eroding silt and clay, Ah-Shi-Sle-Pah Wilderness Study Area   TOM TILL

A haunting reminder of early Pueblo Indian life, Bandelier National Monument   ED COOPER

A stretch of the Wild and Scenic Rio Grande near the Colorado border WILLARD CLAY

Livestock roaming the sagebrush flats near Socorro   WILLIAM B. FOLSOM

66 This is the paradox of the dry lands. They have the outward appearance of being hostile to living things. They impose obstacles, adversities, a harsh environment. They make it hard going for plants, for animals, for people. But in the very act of so doing they make life more worth while. They emphasize its value. They demand from it extra vitality and endurance. They encourage the development of independence and individuality. 99

Jack Schaefer,
States of the Nation: New Mexico

57,000-acre Bosque del Apache National Wildlife Refuge, south of Socorro   JEFF FOOTT

Greater sandhill cranes, brought back from near-extinction at Bosque del Apache   GLENN VAN NIMWEGEN

Airborne sandhill cranes, one of about three hundred bird species at Bosque del Apache   TIM DAVIS

Snow geese, which gather in flocks of as many as fifty thousand in late fall at Bosque del Apache   GLENN VAN NIMWEGEN

> **"** *Nothing is taken for granted. Each ant, each lizard, each lark is imbued with great value simply because the creature is there, simply because the creature is alive in a place where any life at all is precious.... One look and you know that simply to be able to survive is a great triumph, that every possible resource is needed, every possible ally— even the most humble insect or reptile. You realize you will be speaking with all of them if you intend to last out the year.* **"**

Leslie Marmon Silko,
"Landscape, History, and the Pueblo Imagination,"
Antaeus

Fiery flowers of the fishhook barrel cactus   JOHN W. FARRELL

Brilliant scarlet blooms of the claret cup cactus, south of Chaco Canyon   FRED HIRSCHMANN

Vicious spines of the aptly named horse crippler cactus, Living Desert State Park   SCOTT T. SMITH

Casting at Shidoni Foundry and Sculpture Gardens, Tesuque   STEPHEN SIMPSON

They're off at the State Fairgrounds in Albuquerque   KEN GALLARD

An oil-rig technician working in Carlsbad   BUDDY MAYS

A lively game at the Santa Fe Polo Grounds   KEN GALLARD

Farolitos, known as *luminarias* in southern New Mexico, arranged in the shape of a Christmas tree in Taos   RANDALL K. ROBERTS

Farolitos topping a Santa Fe hotel   KEN GALLARD

Carnival lights at the State Fair in Albuquerque   BUDDY MAYS

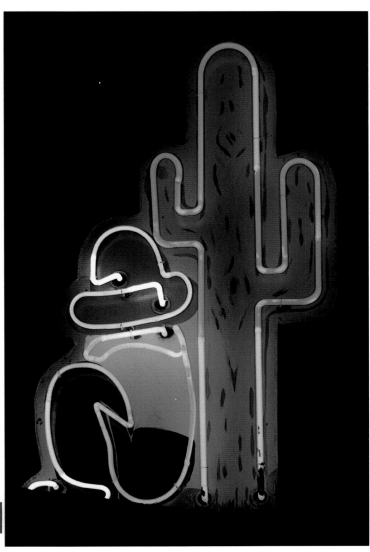

Neon art in Tucumcari   TERRENCE MOORE

Sunset washing the Sacramento Mountains with flame, near White Sands   ROB BADGER

Enchanted Mesa, called Katzimo, or "the accursed," by the nearby Indians of Acoma Pueblo   STEPHEN TRIMBLE

> **❝** *...the moment I saw the brilliant, proud morning shine high up over the deserts...something stood still in my soul, and I started to attend. There was a certain magnificence in the high-up day, a certain eagle-like royalty....For a greatness of beauty I have never experienced anything like New Mexico.* **❞**

D.H. Lawrence,
Phoenix: The Posthumous Papers of D. H. Lawrence

Porch of the Laughing Horse Inn, Taos   ROB BADGER / NITA WINTER

Islamic mosque near Abiquiu   STEPHEN SIMPSON

Folk art decorating an attorney's office in Santa Fe   STEPHEN SIMPSON

A blood-red sunset reflected on a Santa Fe hotel   JAMES BLACK

Swirling dancers at Taos Intertribal Powwow   KEN GALLARD

Drummers at a Deer Dance, Santa Clara Pueblo   STEPHEN TRIMBLE

66 When you attend (a Pueblo dance), you will be at first a trifle bewildered by the sheer mass, then fascinated by the costumes, the color, the music. Shortly after this you will find the performance monotonous, the sun hot, the ground hard, the dust annoying. This is the point at which many people leave. If you stay on, and if you keep quiet, the rhythms of drum, song, and dance, the endlessly changing formations of the lines of dancers, the very heat and dust, unite and take hold. You will realize slowly that what looked simple is complex, disciplined, sophisticated. You will forget yourself. The chances are then you will go away with that same odd, empty, satisfied feeling which comes after absorbing any great work of art. 99

Oliver La Farge,
Holiday

San Jose de Gracia, Las Trampas, one of the finest surviving eighteenth-century churches in the state   DAVID MUENCH

“ The spirit of religion, the sense of layered history, the enormous beauty of landscape under the blue and white sky and the starry darkness, a land of many-cultured richness lived in for at least a millennium and yet still sparsely peopled—these are some of the essences that northern New Mexico holds for me and which I find nowhere else on earth. Land of enchantment, land of nourishment, land of many good returns. ”

Lawrence Clark Powell,
Southwest Review

Palace of the Governors, Santa Fe, oldest continuously used public building in the nation   DAVID MUENCH

Limestone formation known as Temple of the Sun, in the Big Room of Carlsbad Cavern   DAVID MUENCH

Frozen Waterfall, a flowstone deposit at Carlsbad Caverns National Park   JOHN LEMKER / ANIMALS ANIMALS

Dripstone stalagmites in the Deep Secrets Room, Lechuguilla Cave, Carlsbad Caverns   LAURENCE PARENT

Frost gracing ground cover along the road through Taos Canyon   R. J. RIGGE

Yarrow and junipers below Truchas Peak, at 13,102 feet the second highest in the state   WILLARD CLAY

Lower Falls in Frijoles Canyon, Bandelier National Monument   GEORGE H. H. HUEY

Poisonous amanita mushrooms on Greenie Peak in the Sangre de Cristo Mountains   WILLARD CLAY

Valle Grande, ranch country west of Los Alamos   JOHN ELK III

“ *The Pueblo homeland is shaped by the mountains that surround it. For untold centuries, the horizon circle of blue mountains has been the image in every individual's life of the limits of knowing and being and imagining. The mountains, as the rim of a sacred world, have been the collectors and transmitters, not of radio waves, but of the blessings and prayers of the cosmos.*

In the Pueblo homeland, to borrow a phrase from Willa Cather, the sky is not so much the roof of the earth as the earth is a floor for the sky. ”

William deBuys,
Enchantment and Exploitation

Calling it quits for the day   TERRENCE MOORE

Navajo horses roaming the sagebrush desert of Chaco Canyon   STEPHEN TRIMBLE

Ranching in the blood, Bell Ranch, Solano   MATT BRADLEY

Just kids near Artesia   BUDDY MAYS

Riding off into a western sunset BUDDY MAYS

The country below Acoma Pueblo, "The Sky City"   STEPHEN TRIMBLE

" *I know what they tell you about the desert but you mustn't believe them. This is no deathbed. Dig down, the earth is moist. Boulders have turned to dust here, the dust feels like graphite. You can hear a man breathe at a distance of twenty yards. You can see out there to the edge where the desert stops and the mountains begin. You think it is perhaps ten miles. It is more than a hundred. Just before the sun sets all the colors will change. Green will turn to blue, red to gold.* "

Barry Lopez,
Desert Notes

Mountain lion   DENNIS HENRY

Canyon wren   ROBERT C. SIMPSON

Agave struggling to exist in a landscape of lava HENRY H. HOLDSWORTH

" *That land was not empty and dead. It was alive—alive with a strange and strong vitality that made the green-cloaked monotony of eastern landscapes seem mild and pallid. Color was one of the secrets. The deep clear blue of the sky. . . . The dark glowering browns and blacks of ancient lava flows. . . . The sudden brave green of a single plant, alone and with no near nieghbors, seeming to say: Look. Here I am. I've done it. All by myself I've done it. Do you know how wonderful it is to be alive?* "

Jack Schaefer,
States of the Nation: New Mexico

An April display of bladderpods in the San Simon Valley, southwestern New Mexico   JEFF GNASS

The face of the agave, in the Organ Mountains   WILLARD CLAY

The formidable cholla cactus, Pecos National Monument   GEORGE H. H. HUEY

The Comanche Dance, San Ildefonso Pueblo Feast Day   STEPHEN TRIMBLE

Matachine dancer at El Rancho   STEPHEN SIMPSON

San Juan Pueblo boy painted for the Comanche Dance   STEPHEN TRIMBLE

Participant in the Taos Intertribal Powwow   KEN GALLARD

Multicolored Pueblo corn—each with distinctive flavor and ceremonial use   STEPHEN TRIMBLE

Morning sun slipping into a box canyon at El Morro National Monument   JEFF GNASS

Kit fox   DENNIS HENRY

The wandering Chama River near Abiquiu   STEPHEN SIMPSON

Mountain lion cub   DENNIS & MARIA HENRY

Moonrise over Painted Cave. Bandelier National Monument   SCOTT T. SMITH

" *The sudden start and strength of winds here make one feel the facts of astronomy. In cozier country it seems that the sun rises and sets, the moon rises and sets, above a still and level world. But here, as on a great ship, you are more aware of the voyaging planet—the mountains wheeling upward to the sun, and the winds like encountered currents breaking across the turning earth.* "

Winfield Townley Scott,
Exiles and Fabrications

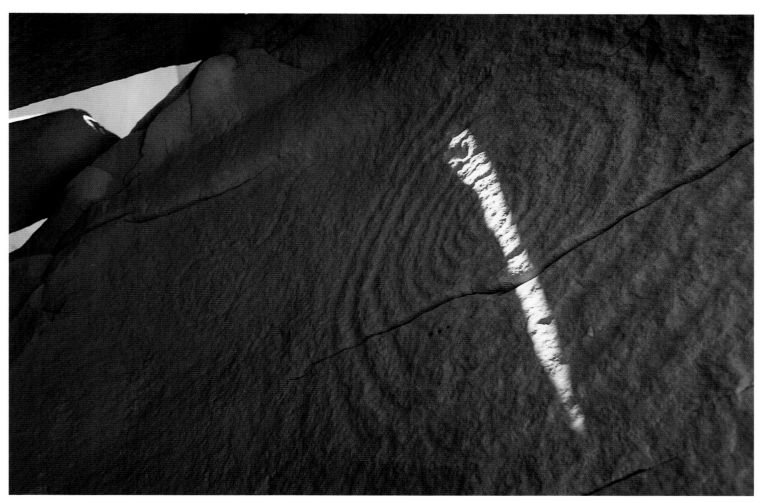

The Sundagger, a Chaco-Anasazi formation which, until 1990, marked the solstices and equinoxes   BARBARA BRUNDEGE / EUGENE FISHER

The Very Large Array radio telescope, west of Socorro   ROB BADGER

Albuquerque at night, from the summit of Sandia Peak   TOM BEAN

Sunset over Bluewater Lake State Park, west of Grants   ROBERT WINSLOW

" *The whole western sky was the colour of golden ashes, with here and there a flush of red on the lip of a little cloud.* "

Willa Cather,
Death Comes for the Archbishop

Fort Union National Monument north of Las Vegas, established in 1851 on the Santa Fe Trail   STEWART M. GREEN

Abandoned farmhouse and windmill on the plains near Raton   WILLARD CLAY

Remains of the once-rowdy mining town of Mogollon, in southwestern New Mexico   ED COOPER

Maples beginning to dress for fall in the Gila Wilderness, oldest national forest wilderness in the nation   LAURENCE PARENT

Autumn on the 1.7-million-acre Santa Fe National Forest   TERRENCE MOORE

" *Autumn, with its sad and mystifying alchemy of death; autumn, that colorful deciduous time of year when leaves tumble off cottonwoods, elms, and aspens in great clattering sheaves, skittering among chickens and dry papery cornstalks, gathering in crisp drifts against the firewalls of dirt roofs. A southern sun, dead leaves, and smoke heralded the end of another brief season.* "

John Nichols,
The Magic Journey

Snowcovered *hornos,* ovens in which bread is baked at Taos Pueblo   DAVID MUENCH

Sunset warming a winter day at El Morro National Monument   FRED HIRSCHMANN

La Ventana Natural Arch, El Malpais National Conservation Area   TOM BEAN

We do not destroy or disturb the harmony of nature. To us this is beauty; it is our sense of esthetics. We care for and husband our environment. We feel ourselves trustees of our environment and of our creative values. And this gives us a union with all existence.

Popovi Da,
quoted in The Pueblo Indians

Roadrunner, the state bird   JOE McDONALD

A solitary sycamore in the Gila Wilderness, one of the largest national forest wildernesses in the nation   PETER KRESAN

A table mesa on the far horizon, northwestern New Mexico   DAVID MUENCH

> **The breadth and height of the land, its huge self and its huge sky, strike you like a blow.**
>
> Winfield Townley Scott,
> Exiles and Fabrications

Coneflowers near Alamogordo   BUDDY MAYS

Colorful Indian blankets   JAMES O. SNEDDON

Mountain bluebird   LARRY R. DITTO

Sun and ice illuminating a ponderosa pine, El Morro National Monument   FRED HIRSCHMANN

Ice Cave, one of several intriguing lava-tube caves at El Malpais National Monument   FRED HIRSCHMANN

" *I think New Mexico was the greatest experience from the outside world that I have ever had. It certainly changed me for ever. Curious as it may sound, it was New Mexico that liberated me from the present era of civilization, the great era of material and mechanical development.* **"**

D.H. Lawrence,
Phoenix

Sandstone bluffs, El Malpais National Conservation Area   RANDALL K. ROBERTS

they made it possible

New Mexico on my Mind would have been impossible to produce without the creative and technical skills of more than fifty professional photographers. These men and women succeeded in a difficult task—capturing the many moods and faces of New Mexico.

From majestic landscapes to delicate *luminarias*, New Mexico contains a breathtaking array of beautiful images, but transforming these images onto film requires more than just a camera. It takes an eye for composition, technical expertise, long hours of work, and the sheer determination to obtain a memorable shot rather than a mere snapshot.

The photographers for *New Mexico on my Mind* provided this extra skill and effort. They hiked, climbed, waited, and watched to get the best possible images from all parts of the state.

To all the excellent photographers who contributed to *New Mexico on my Mind*, thank you.

The Globe Pequot Press

Photographers in *New Mexico on my Mind*

Rob Badger
Tom Bean
Greg Ryan-Sally Beyer
James Black
Matt Bradley
Barbara Brundege
Willard Clay
Ed Cooper
Kent & Donna Dannen
Tim Davis
Larry R. Ditto
John Elk III
John W. Farrell
Eugene Fisher
William B. Folsom
Jeff Foott
Ken Gallard
Jeff Gnass
Stewart M. Green
Dennis Henry
Maria Henry
Fred Hirschmann
Henry H. Holdsworth
George H. H. Huey
Peter Kresan
John Lemker
Donald N. Leske
Robert Lienemann

Buddy Mays
Joe McDonald
Suzi S. Moore
Terrence Moore
David Muench
Hiram L. Parent
Laurence Parent
Brian Parker
Chuck Place
R. J. Rigge
Randall K. Roberts
Ron Sanford
Robert C. Simpson
Stephen Simpson
Scott T. Smith
James O. Sneddon
Tom Till
Stephen Trimble
Larry Ulrich
Glenn Van Nimwegen
Jan L. Wassink
Robert Winslow
Nita Winter
Edward Worman
Agencies
  Animals/Animals
  Portfolio
  Tom Stack & Associates

acknowledgements

The publishers gratefully acknowledge the following sources:

Pages 10 and 47 from *Ernie Pyle's Southwest* by Ernie Pyle. Copyright © 1965 by Desert-Southwest, Inc., Publishers.

Pages 12 and 101 from *Death Comes for the Archbishop* by Willa Cather. Copyright © 1955 by the Executors of the Estate of Willa Cather. Published 1967 by Alfred A. Knopf, Inc.

Page 15 from a letter from Georgia O'Keeffe to Alfred Stieglitz, Sept. 20, 1937. Published originally in 1937-38 exhibition catalog. Reprinted in *Portrait of an Artist* by Laurie Lisle. Copyright © 1980 by the author.

Pages 20 and 108 from *The Pueblo Indians* by Joe S. Sando. Copyright © 1976 by The Indian Historical Press, Inc.

Page 24 from *America the Beautiful: New Mexico* by R. Conrad Stein. Copyright © 1988 by Regensteiner Publishing Enterprise, Inc. Published by Chicago Children's Press.

Page 30 from *New Mexico Quarterly* 27, no. 3, Autumn 1957.

Page 32 from *Far From Cibola* by Paul Horgan. Copyright © 1936 by Paul Horgan. Published 1974 by the University of New Mexico Press.

Page 41 from *If Mountains Die: A New Mexico Memoir* by John Nichols. Copyright © 1979 by John Nichols and William Davis. Published by Alfred A. Knopf, Inc.

Page 49 from *The Land of Little Rain* by Mary Austin. Copyright © 1903. Published 1974 by the University of New Mexico Press.

Pages 55 and 88 from *States of the Nation: New Mexico* by Jack Schaefer. Copyright © 1967 by the author. Published by Coward-McCann, Inc.

Page 59 from "Landscape, History, and the Pueblo Imagination," *Antaeus* 57, Autumn 1986.

Pages 67 and 116 from *Phoenix: The Posthumous Papers of D. H. Lawrence*, edited by Edward D. McDonald. Copyright © 1936 by Frieda Lawrence. Published by The Viking Press.

Page 71 from *Holiday*. Copyright © 1952 by The Curtis Publishing Co.

Page 72 from *Southwest Review*. Copyright © 1957 by Southern Methodist University Press.

Page 81 from *Enchantment and Exploitation* by William deBuys. Copyright © 1985 by the author. Published by the University of New Mexico Press.

Page 86 from *Desert Notes: Reflections in the Eye of a Raven* by Barry Holstun Lopez. Copyright © 1976 by the author. Published by Avon Books, a division of The Hearst Corp.

Pages 98 and 111 from *Exiles and Fabrications* by Winfield Townley Scott. Copyright © 1961 by the author. Published by Doubleday & Co., Inc.

Page 105 from *The Magic Journey* by John Nichols. Copyright © 1978 by the author. Published by Ballantine Books.

About Jim Arnholz

Jim Arnholz was born in Chicago and grew up in the Midwest. He came to New Mexico in 1967 while in the Air Force and soon became a New Mexican by "passionate adoption." Upon his discharge in 1970, he enrolled at the University of New Mexico, graduating in 1973 and going to work at the *Las Cruces Sun-News*. He has been with the *Albuquerque Journal* for thirteen years, working as a copy editor, assistant city editor, feature editor, and, since 1981, columnist.

Last brush stroke of the day in Taos BUDDY MAYS